no

vestments

e made to reduce

capita water consumption

hen **36** states in the U.S.

030 then **640,000** new

ctares (**18,500** acres) of industrial land

44% then Italy's potential labor force will

6 million (**21%**) will be over **65** years old and **34**

2 units per acre and located in mixed-use neighborhoods **then**

owth of greenhouse gas emissions would be reduced **7–10%**. **if** the

ople **then** its population will have tripled. **if** economic trends in

uld grow from **15%** of the G6 countries to greater than the

en past trends suggest that **72** million will be built

mate change **then** disastrous impacts can be

n to **750** ppm **then** sea level rise will

er **65** years old in Italy grows by

4% **then** Italy's

tential labor force

ll decline by

2%.

Tl

2050:

Creating
Blueprints
for
Change

The Urban Land Institute gratefully acknowledges the support of the City in 2050 initiative by a founding grant from the **Galbreath Family Foundation** in the memory of John W. Galbreath and Daniel M. Galbreath.

Galbreath Family Foundation

The Urban Land Institute gratefully acknowledges the additional financial support of the production of this publication by Cherokee and the following sponsors in the underwriting of the exhibition.

ULI—the Urban Land Institute is a 501(c) (3) nonprofit research and education organization supported by its members. Founded in 1936, the Institute now has more than 40,000 members worldwide representing the entire spectrum of land use and real estate development disciplines, working in private enterprise and public service.

As the preeminent, multidisciplinary real estate forum, ULI facilitates the open exchange of ideas, information, and experience among local, national, and international industry leaders and policy makers dedicated to creating better places.

The mission of the Urban Land Institute is to provide leadership in the responsible use of land and in creating and sustaining thriving communities worldwide. ULI is committed to

□ Bringing together leaders from across the fields of real estate and land use policy to exchange best practices and serve community needs;
□ Fostering collaboration within and beyond ULI's membership through mentoring, dialogue, and problem-solving;
□ Exploring issues of urbanization, conservation, regeneration, land use, capital formation, and sustainable development;
□ Advancing land use policies and design practices that respect the uniqueness of both built and natural environments;
□ Sharing knowledge through education, applied research, publishing, and electronic media; and
□ Sustaining a diverse global network of local practice and advisory efforts that address current and future challenges.

Foreword

For many years, the Urban Land Institute has showcased best practices in land development that accommodate population growth while preserving land resources. This continues to be a fundamental activity in the Institute's mission to provide leadership in the responsible use of land and in creating and sustaining thriving communities worldwide. With over 40,000 members in over 90 countries, ULI is a source of creative change to encourage the early adoption of the best ideas in urban development.

The recent instability of global capital markets creates yet another imperative for ULI. Real estate markets will be restructured and regulatory frameworks redefined. ULI's mission calls us to forge ahead and proactively explore new land use paradigms and scenarios. This is a crucial time to help land use professionals innovate and explore new business strategies.

With *The City in 2050: Creating Blueprints for Change*, we take the opportunity to create a dialogue that explores potential paths of innovation. The initiative is being presented as an exchange of ideas to prepare for and act upon the changes facing metropolitan areas over the next decades as the world becomes more urbanized.

Elevated concerns over capital markets, rising energy costs, climate change, exploding populations, and equitable development are changing how communities define "the responsible use of land." As these issues increasingly affect our daily lives, discussions regarding sustainable development continue to both broaden and escalate.

In only 42 years, when we mark the midpoint of the 21st century, cities around the world will have experienced unprecedented growth—serving larger and more diverse populations than ever in world history. The quest to balance market pressures, public policy goals, and land use decisions in a fast-paced global marketplace will be more challenging than ever.

Already, we see a rising wave of innovation responding to new markets, technologies, and regulations. How will land use professionals help guide public and private investment to best achieve attractive returns and long-term sustained value? And how should communities and investors act to meet their needs while empowering future generations to meet theirs?

The issue of climate change is one of the most important and complex long-term challenges ever faced by communities around the world and land use professionals have a huge stake in finding solutions to address it. Although cutting energy consumption in buildings is a big part of the answer, locating land uses to reduce vehicle miles traveled and harnessing clean sources of energy are

In only 42 years, when we mark the midpoint of the 21st century, cities around the world will have experienced unprecedented growth—serving larger and more diverse populations than ever in world history.

The drive toward 2050 is about building sustainable communities that withstand the test of time. It is about building for people and about building in harmony with the natural environment—not in spite of it.

critical to success. Whether in storm-prone or high-risk locations or at the urban edge, sustainable development practices must go beyond green buildings.

In the U.S. alone, at least two-thirds of the buildings that will be needed by 2050 are not yet built and as much as 80 percent of urban development is projected to be located at the "edge" of metropolitan areas. The linkage between land use patterns and climate change strategies makes the strongest case ever for building more efficiently throughout urban regions, particularly in newly developing communities. Well-planned communities—those that give residents the option to drive only a short distance, walk, bike, or take transit—have a central role to play in mitigating climate change.

The 2008 ULI Fall Meeting in Miami commences this interdisciplinary conversation on alternative "blueprints" which get us to 2050. As the dialogue about the environment and sustainable development goes mainstream, we are observing a shift in the public mind-set about how and where people want to live, and how they would like to get from one place to another. In fact, it is quite possible that globally, communities are in the midst of redefining both living and working patterns, an evolution catalyzed by new technologies as well as "kitchen table" decisions related to traffic congestion, gasoline costs, and carbon footprints.

The drive toward 2050 is about building sustainable communities that withstand the test of time. It is about building for people and about building in harmony with the natural environment—not in spite of it. *The City in 2050* will be informed by the work of ULI's other policy initiatives and will disseminate useful information from around the globe that showcases best practices, innovative strategies, and blueprints that address pressing urban development challenges.

We hope *The City in 2050* will stimulate an ongoing dialogue which fosters new models of practice for the future.

Richard M. Rosan
President, ULI Worldwide

How can ci
communitie
shaped to n
present nee
empowerin
future gene
to meet the

es and
 be
et
s while

ations
s?

Capital Markets Concentration of Capital

Institutional investors and niche players grow in importance and define larger segments of the market.

Capital Markets Competition for Capital

Cities and regions vie for investment in a global marketplace.

Capital Markets Assessing Value and Risk

The speed of the marketplace and new economic inputs make the assessment and pricing of risk more difficult.

CASH...FAST!
800-249-5827
SellYourHouseQuickOnline.com

SECURITY CAMERA

Climate Change Climbing Temperatures

Cities that currently experience heat waves are expected to be challenged by an increased number, intensity, and duration of heat waves during the course of the century.

Climate Change Severe Weather

Changing weather patterns place higher burdens on infrastructure, such as power lines, sewer systems, levees, and coastal evacuation routes.

Climate Change Rising Seas

Many millions more people are projected to experience floods every year due to sea level rise. The numbers affected will be the largest in the densely populated, low-lying mega-deltas of Asia and Africa.

Infrastructure Deferred Maintenance

Underinvestment and deferred maintenance can result in tragic consequences.

Infrastructure Communication Networks

Interconnected global systems create new economic opportunities, but introduce operational risks.

Infrastructure Unsustainable Patterns

Both capital and operational costs are higher for infrastructure in low-density communities.

Water Vulnerable Sources

Many semi-arid and arid areas
such as the Mediterranean Basin,
western USA, southern Africa, and
northeastern Brazil are projected to
suffer a decrease of water resources
due to climate change.

Water Diminishing Reserves

The availability of clean sources
of water complicates the economic
growth of communities and
regions worldwide.

Water Pollution Runoff

Persistent waterborne pollution knows
no political boundaries.

Energy Reducing Emissions

The need to reduce greenhouse gas emissions creates dynamic market conditions in the energy sector.

Energy Peaking Oil

Rising gas prices have reduced vehicle-miles traveled in the U.S. for the first time in 30 years.

Energy Security Risks

Seventy percent of oil consumed in the United States is imported from other countries.

Demographics Growing Populations

World population is projected to rise
to 9 billion by 2050, with seven of every
ten people living in urban areas.

Demographics Regional Migrations

Economic competitiveness will "push"
and "pull" migration between regions.

Demographics Shifting Demographics

Demographic shifts in age, ethnicity,
and household composition will create
new markets and drive tensions
between "haves" and "have-nots."

What must
now to crea
the City of

ve do

e value in

)50?

Weaving together regional water management, habitat protection, and recreation, the Xochimilco park outside Mexico City has put Mexican landscape design on the international map.

Falcons in New York City, salmon in Seattle, manatee in Miami—the drama of urban life extends into nature. Reengineered waterfronts, new forests, and restored stream valleys are shaping new addresses for urban development. The fringe benefit? Green infrastructure can reduce the need for costly traditional infrastructure.

Diamonds, Emeralds, and Sapphires

"Meet me at Park Café!" By reclaiming "leftover" urban spaces, developers create coveted destinations that become landmarks and peaceful escapes from bustling urban streets. Access to shade, water features, paths, and trails give residents an opportunity to engage the many dimensions of nature.

Growing Capacity

Investment in green infrastructure is happening in neighborhoods once overlooked. New investments can be leveraged to create green jobs and increase social equity. The greening of cities represents an opportunity to broaden the workforce and engage communities that have not benefited from past growth. Educating new generations in the responsibilities of stewardship will help meet global environmental challenges.

Serious Green

As investments in water and air quality move beyond "pipes and pumps," the regional green infrastructure plan becomes a central strategy for managing growth. Regional parks are more than protection of habitat or mitigation of pollution and heat-island effects. Building on rich traditions—from English gardens to Olmsted parks to reclaimed waterfronts—green infrastructure will reconnect us to nature and to each other.

Extreme Makeovers

Large parks are being financed by a new generation of urban development. Whether reclaiming brownfield sites or building new town centers, urban development integrates place-making designs with phasing plans. Large parks give projects the focus and identity to become vital neighborhoods, even as construction continues for decades. Value is created, quality of life is established, and residential units are sold.

Competitive Green

Breathing the cleanest air, drinking the purest water, having the most vital stream—when competing for jobs in the global marketplace, quality of life will rule. Cities will compete to be the most environmentally friendly place to live, work, and play—and green will be a central element of their brand. Green metrics will draw new residents, events, and corporations.

1 Even before its completion, the Highline Project has been critical to the redevelopment of the Chelsea neighborhood in Manhattan. Like Millennium Park in Chicago, this new public space will offer a unique park experience in the middle of the city.

2 The urban development plans for the London 2012 Olympics will channel investment into overlooked neighborhoods. Brownfield remediation, river restoration, and the creation of neighborhood jobs and affordable housing are all targeted outcomes.

3 The restoration of the L.A. River in Los Angeles, California, will transform the concrete basin into a dynamic green space with bioengineered habitats and recreation elements, reconnecting neighborhoods long cut off from one another.

4 High-rise development built in tandem with new urban open space in Milan, Italy, benefits from access to green space, prestige of address, and increased values.

5 Quality of life for workers and neighborhood residents alike will drive competitiveness decisions between regions and cities.

Local and State Measures for Land Conservation in the U.S.

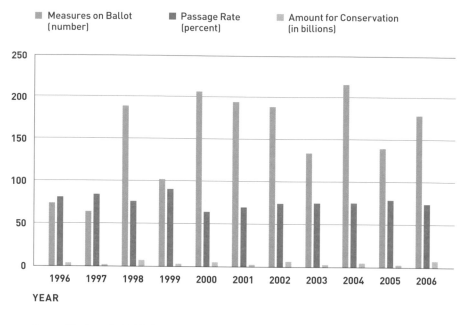

- Measures on Ballot (number)
- Passage Rate (percent)
- Amount for Conservation (in billions)

YEAR

Source: The Trust for Public Land, 2007

Top Ten Most Visited City Parks in the U.S.

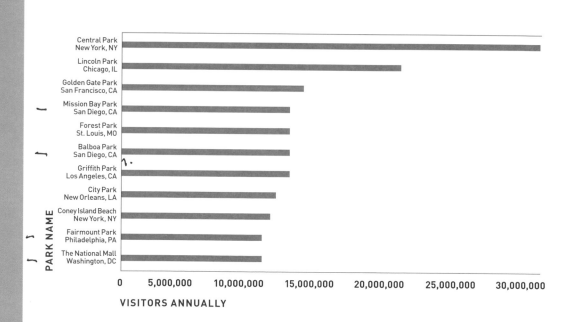

Central Park
New York, NY

Lincoln Park
Chicago, IL

Golden Gate Park
San Francisco, CA

Mission Bay Park
San Diego, CA

Forest Park
St. Louis, MO

Balboa Park
San Diego, CA

Griffith Park
Los Angeles, CA

City Park
New Orleans, LA

Coney Island Beach
New York, NY

Fairmount Park
Philadelphia, PA

The National Mall
Washington, DC

PARK NAME

VISITORS ANNUALLY

Source: The Trust for Public Land, 2007

Park-Related Spending per Capita for Select U.S. Cities

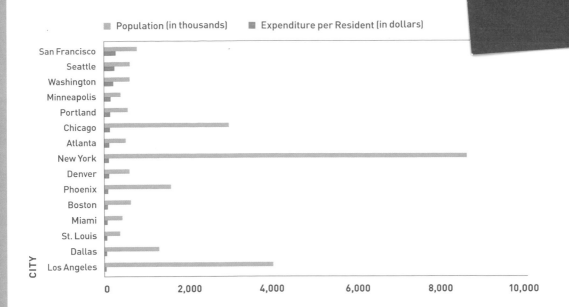

■ Population (in thousands)   ■ Expenditure per Resident (in dollars)

Source: The Trust for Public Land, Fiscal Year 2006

Total Parkland as a Percent of City Land Area for Select U.S. Cities

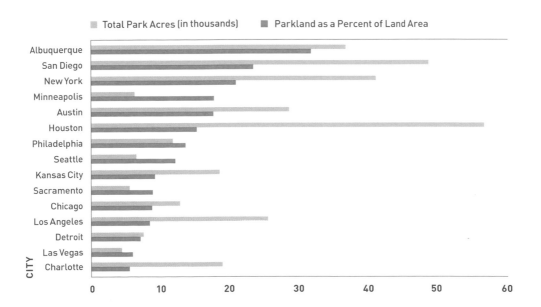

■ Total Park Acres (in thousands)   ■ Parkland as a Percent of Land Area

Source: The Trust for Public Land, 2007

Water, Powe

The 214-turbine King Mountain Wind Ranch in Texas has a 278.2-megawatt (MW) capacity, of which 76.7 megawatts are purchased and used by the city of Austin to power 55,000 homes.

Light.

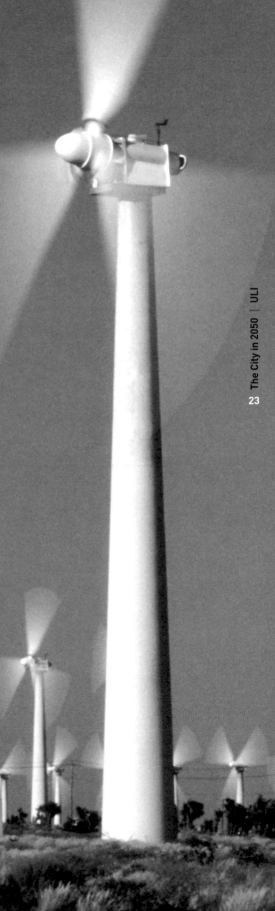

Infrastructure—the lifeline of thriving cities—is undergoing big changes. The worldwide quest to reduce greenhouse gas emissions is driving new economies. Decentralized and alternative technologies will enable new design solutions. Higher energy and water prices will induce investment and alter behavior patterns. Entrepreneurial investment will forge new business relationships.

Water, Power, **Light.**

24

How will the infrastructure be phased?   Is land value financing transit?

Elevating Water

Where there's water, there's life—and urban development potential. The rising scarcity of adequate water supplies requires a reevaluation of sources, the management of consumption, and deployment of conservation technologies. Low-impact development will promote water recycling and recharge aquifers; new landscapes will no longer rely on irrigation; and green roofs and bioswales will passively clean water pollutants.

Staying in Touch

Telecommunications stands next to energy and water as a community essential. How will we communicate with one another in 2050? How will even more information drive lifestyle choices? Increasing speed and complexity are a sure bet. As buildings and cars learn to "talk" through interactive networks, the lives of users will be empowered with new alternatives and performance-based outcomes.

1 Completed in 2005, the Ashkelon Water Desalination Plant in Israel produces 13 percent of the country's domestic consumer demand—equivalent to nearly 6 percent of Israel's total water needs.

2 At a time when telecom is becoming increasingly wireless—even invisible—the monumental communications tower in Barcelona, Spain, underscores the significant infrastructure investment demanded by these evolving technologies.

3 Hanham Hall, a 200-unit development, is slated to become one of the first zero-carbon communities in the U.K. It will use energy metering and below-ground heat recovery technology to recycle heat used by each unit.

4 Federal and state incentives as well as increasing public demand are making solar power an affordable, energy-efficient choice for developers.

5 Located in San Diego County, California, the Alvarado Water Treatment Plant sets a new sustainable precedent by featuring a green roof and a 1-megawatt (MW) solar power system that produces 20 percent of the plant's electricity.

Transparency, Feedback, Control

Reducing costs means finding efficiencies and eliminating waste. Smart meters will relay the consumption patterns of energy and water to encourage user behavior adjustments. Just as we monitor cell phone minutes today, energy meters, smart networks, and information alerts will inform consumers and empower building managers to make real-time adjustments.

Sources and Uses

The drive toward a low-carbon economy will diversify power sources and restructure electricity transmission. New options to buy and sell energy—including avoided consumption—make real estate a central player. As new economic frameworks create new feasibility, power generation and urban development will find synergies and revenue opportunities.

Outputs Are Inputs

Building demolition and construction produce 20 percent of all landfill waste in the United States. Recycling materials, buildings, and contaminated brownfields will further develop an economy of reuse. Communities will harvest methane from landfills. Recycled as compost, organic wastes will support urban agriculture—creating a cost-effective, less distribution-intensive food supply.

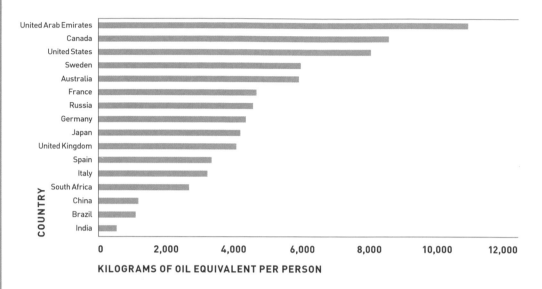

Energy Consumption per Capita

Source: World Resources Institute, 2003

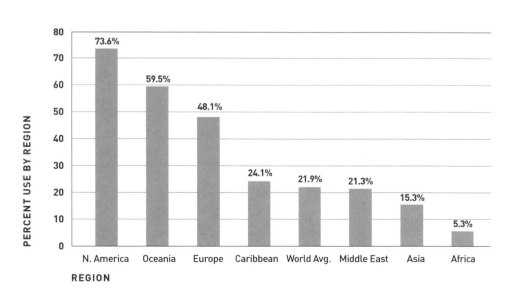

Internet Use by Geographic Region, 2008

Source: Internet World Stats, Miniwatts Marketing Group

Global Water Consumption 1900–2025

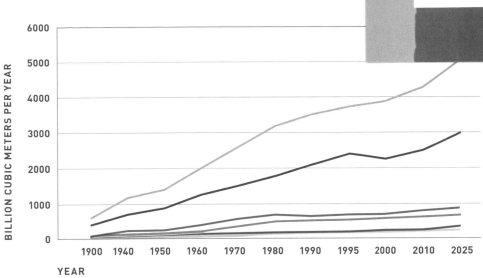

Source: Federal Environment Agency of Germany

Traffic Congestion in the U.S.: Use Has Far Outpaced Road Construction

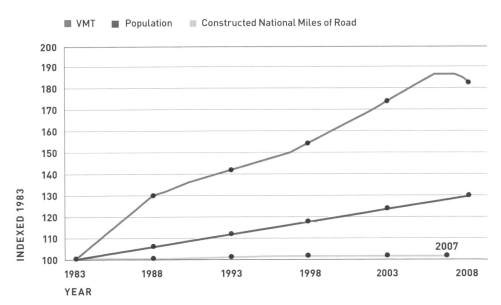

This chart would look different with more compact development.

Source: Federal Highway Administration–Highway Statistics Reports, U.S. Census Bureau–Population Data

etro Metric

Creating Blueprints for Change

Vancouver's 2008 Average Annual Metro Metrics

Population
50% 2.25 million
urban; **50%** metropolitan
1.6% annual growth **52%** non-English as first language
33% are creative professionals
70 languages spoken

Murders **62** per year
Smoking Banned in all bars and restaurants
Last Call **2:00 am**
Vehicles **3** minutes of idling allowed
Homeless **30%** are Aboriginal persons
Homes **$500,000** average p

Households **$49,600** average annual income
18.5% of income spent on transportation
Schools **36%** children walk to school
Recreation Ski, hike, sail on same day

Port **$43** billion in trade
82 million tons of cargo
3 day average container dwell time **Energy** **22%** Hydroelectric
49% Natural Gas
22% Gasoline

Land
50% **28%** of regional land is developed
of developed land is residential
84% of growth is outside of
Vancouver City

Location **38** miles from
Governance **21** U.S. border
municipalities
30% voter turnout of eligible voters
Landfill Waste
641 kg per capita

Airport **872** international flights
per week
Fixed-rail rapid transit
to downtown
Climate **(2009)**
Warmest city in Canada

GHG Emissions **41,013** metric tons from
50% government sources
of that from goods & services
6.3% per capita reduction
(1991–1999)
Economy **57%** of British Columbia GDP
11% is arts and culture **3** rd largest film industry
in North America
4.1% unemployment (2006)

In 2050, the world will be urban, and economic competition will heat up, with Brazil, Russia, India, and China stoking the fire. Two billion people will have joined the middle class, bringing new aspirations and discretionary spending with them. Cities will compete around performance metrics like workforce readiness, emissions reductions, mobility indices, public health, water availability, and geopolitical risk.

Is there a carbon footprint? What is metropolitan congestion priced at? Is

New Rewards

As evolving markets define new risks and rewards, cities that embrace innovation and change will see their fortunes rise. Thriving communities will explore alternatives and make deliberate investments. Bangalore captures IT; Chicago acquires aerospace; Singapore bets on gaming; Abu Dhabi generates renewable energy.

The Good Life: 2050

As market preferences inform consumer choices, people will vote with their feet and transform cities. Whether seeking growth potential, a reasonable cost of living, comfortable climates, or manageable routines, consumers will redefine lifestyle preferences and definitions of the good life.

Get Your Workforce Ready

Metropolitan regions are the engines driving prosperity. With 60 percent of U.S. jobs and 75 percent of economic output located in metro regions, the tissue of human capital will be the baseline of urban vitality. The capacity to care for, train, and invest in citizens will be inextricably linked to prosperity.

Extraordinary Urban Growth

In just 42 years, urban populations will double from 3 to 6 billion people—including 300 million people living in U.S. cities. Unprecedented demand for housing, jobs, and resources can be harnessed to develop new sustainable urban environments. Innovation and prudence will be rewarded. Complacency and negligence will be punished.

Convene, Elevate, Act

Whether financing affordable housing, mitigating pollution, or funding infrastructure, the challenges of metropolitan growth tower over individual political jurisdictions. The effectiveness of regional governance will be measured by fiscal responsibility, consistency, and transparency.

1 Citizens of Seattle, Washington, are developing the local economy by instituting land use models that directly reduce carbon emissions. With its 2030 population projected to increase by 1.7 million people, Seattle stands to benefit from its forward-thinking approach to growth.

2 Adaptive reuse of valued historic structures continues to be a manifestation of community identity.

3 The studying never ends as professional requirements and the definition of the workplace continue to evolve.

4 With over 20 million people, Seoul, South Korea, is directing growth to new towns such as New Songdo City. Located on a waterfront site between the urban core and airport, Songdo City will support 300,000 jobs and 65,000 residents on 1,500 acres (607 ha).

5 After simulating multiple regional growth alternatives, the Sacramento, California, Council of Governments acted to embrace compact land use development that will reduce overall reliance on car travel.

The Future Is Urban

■ In Rural Areas   ■ In Urban Areas

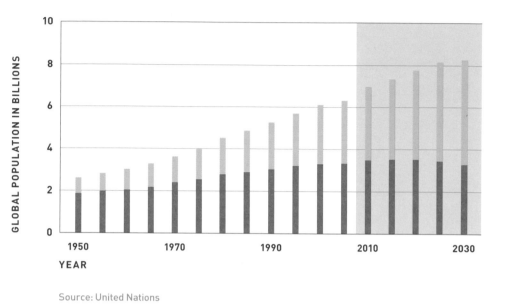

Source: United Nations

Per Capita Carbon Footprints in the U.S.: Emissions per Capita in the 100 Largest Metro Areas

Least ● ● ● ● Most

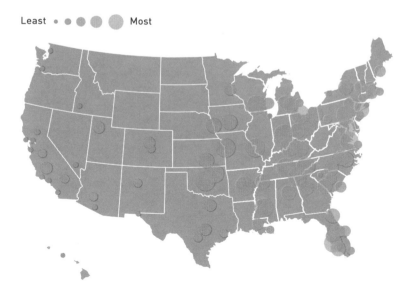

Emissions from the transportation and residential sectors vary by metro area, largely due to how each generates energy.

Source: The Brookings Institution, 2005

Less Is More: California's Annual Electricity Use, 1960–2008

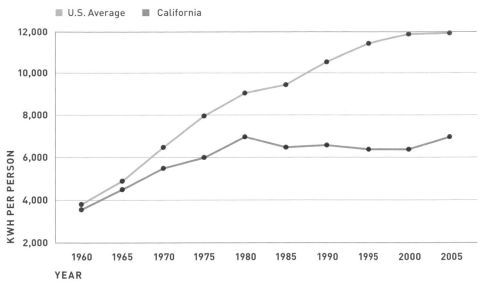

California's per capita electricity use has remained flat since the mid-1970's as a result of aggressive legislation.

Source: *New York Times*

Estimated Vehicle-Miles Traveled by Region in the U.S., May 2008 (in billions) and Percentage Change from 2007

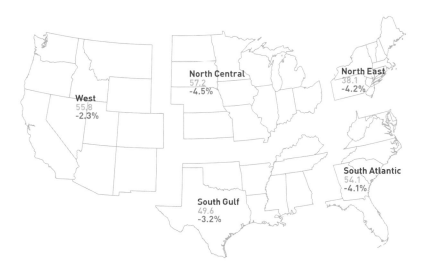

Source: U.S. Department of Transportation, 2008

Whole
Buildings

The Bosco Verticale (Vertical Forest) in Milan, Italy, includes two residential towers whose facades will be completely covered in a variety of flora and utilize on-site wind power.

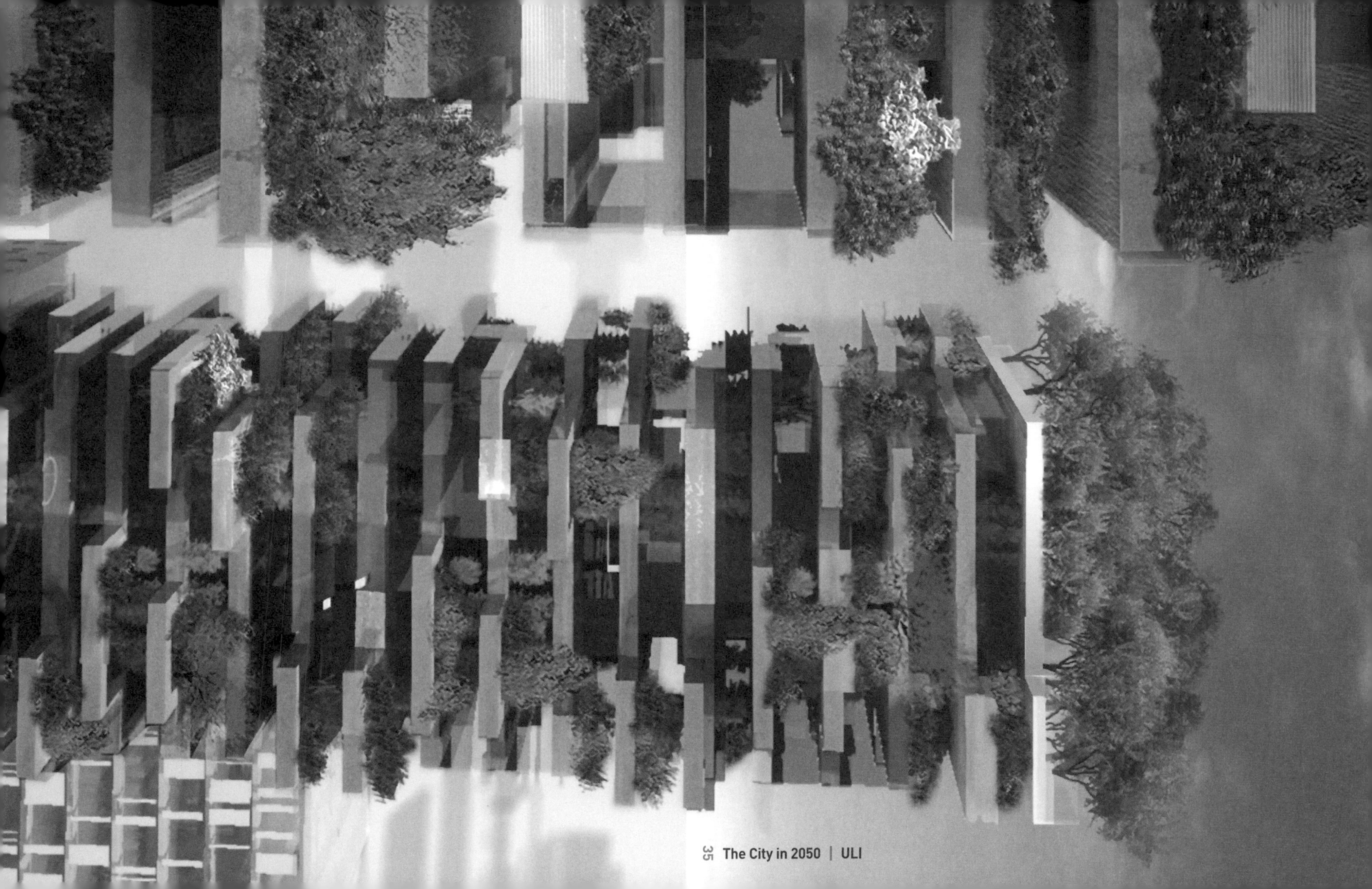

Buildings and their construction account for nearly half of all energy consumed each year. As global population swells by 3 billion people, we will need more buildings than ever— millions more in the United States alone. The challenge to deliver sweeping changes across the entire building stock offers a vast opportunity to reshape our cities for a sustainable future.

What are the life cycle energy costs?   Which building materials cannot b

Giving Back

As architects find ways to design zero-net-energy buildings, energy-positive buildings will be the new leadership standard. This real estate will have energy to spare. The challenge? Design buildings that can keep up with changing land uses and be easily modified with innovative retrofits.

Material Opportunity

The life cycle of building materials cuts across all facets of the economy and the environment. Industrial cycles add up to the total embodied energy of products —and their cumulative impact. How can we reuse what we already have? Whether glass, concrete, or steel, recycling offers bold steps toward sustainability.

Beneficial Occupancy

Human health and wellness are the drivers of productivity and growth. As green building metrics are further refined, the benefits of a building's impact on its occupants will be quantified and valued. Superior air quality, natural daylighting, and user-controlled environments translate into preserving a company's human capital.

A Box Is a Box Is a Box?

After buildings get built, the city around them continues to change. Design innovation will require more than employing the latest technologies—it requires creating spaces that can be reused rather than torn down and rebuilt every 25 years. How will the buildings of today fare in 42 years? Sustainable design will mean flexible in technology and flexible in use.

Systematic Savings

It will take more than a few add-ons to green buildings. Computer simulations allow architects to make integrated decisions that minimize risk. Rapidly evolving technologies— including LED lighting, thermal recovery, variable translucent glass, and many others—allow developers to deliver buildings with enduring performance.

1 Masdar Headquarters will be the first mixed-use, positive-energy building in the zero carbon emission Masdar City outside of Abu Dhabi in the United Arab Emirates.

2 Harvard University's Allston Science Complex will produce half of the greenhouse gas emissions of a typical laboratory building by incorporating photovoltaics and a ground-well geothermal heating and cooling system.

3 Located in Raleigh, North Carolina, Cherokee's new headquarters is an adaptive reuse redevelopment of multiple downtown buildings. The project has documented reductions of both direct and indirect energy consumption.

4 The building of the future will not just sit on a lot. It will be productive. From solar panels that produce power to tree-filled terraces that recycle water, the building will work, literally, from the inside out.

5 The Transbay Transit Center is a visionary transportation and mixed-use project that will transform downtown San Francisco, California, and its regional transportation system by creating a Grand Central Station of the West and a new transit-friendly neighborhood.

How is energy use optimized? Who owns the waste heat?

Energy Used to Operate Buildings Produces 43% of CO_2 Emissions in the U.S.

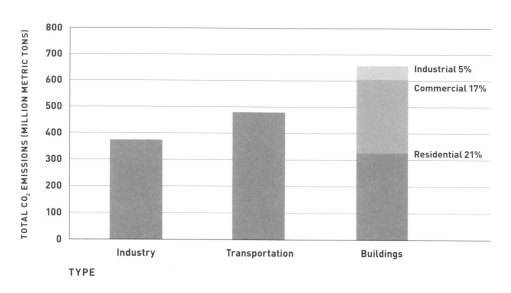

Source: Energy Information Administration, Annual Energy Outlook, 2004

Prices for Construction Materials Soar

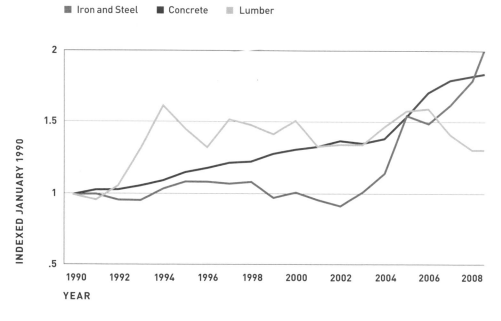

Source: Bureau of Labor Statistics

Energy Consumption by Residential Buildings in the U.S.

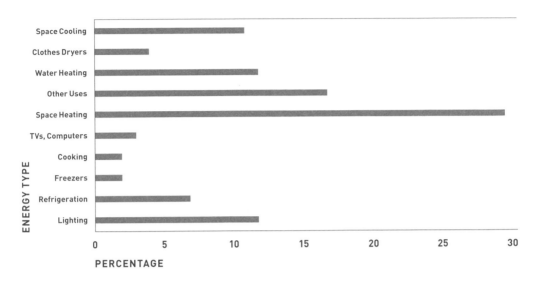

Source: Energy Information Administration, 2002

Average Annual Energy Consumption of Commercial Buildings in the U.S.

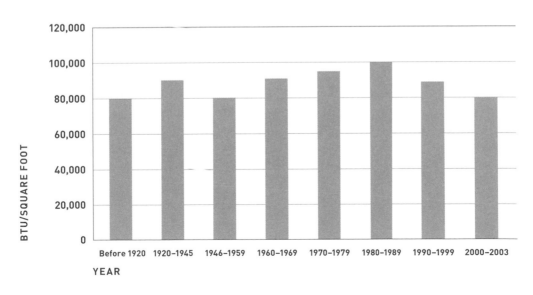

Source: Energy Information Administration, 2003

Getting Arou

40

The proposed City Car is
a stackable electric two-passenger
vehicle that could maximize
scarce urban parking. Innovative
transportation alternatives can
enhance mobility and save money.

New technologies will offer new options—from smaller cars and individualized transit to high-speed rail and smart buses. Moving forward, developers will find tremendous potential to link land use with transportation, creating a larger, more integrated system of choices that promote health, quality of life, and regional competitiveness.

Moving Forward Together

Nearly nine out of ten workers commute by car. Why? Often it's the only option. Transit choices delivered by both public and private sectors will add value and potential profits while new information technologies will add convenience and certainty.

Think Small

Today, 80 percent of five-passenger cars hold only one person 90 percent of the time. But vehicle technologies will profoundly reduce these inefficiencies and affect development. Smaller cars and electric motors will redefine everything from mobility and service centers to zoning.

Choose to Compete

Transportation infrastructure makes or breaks location decisions in today's global economy—always has, always will. To win new business, metropolitan regions will need to offer efficient transportation options connected on a regional, national, and international scale.

First Things First

Where's the golden opportunity in fixing existing transportation infrastructure? By investing in repairs and shrinking America's $1.6 trillion infrastructure deficit, developers can reduce their risk while generating new returns on past investments.

Close Enough?

In the U.S. only 25 percent of all vehicle trips are between work and home. Land use patterns that integrate town centers or mixed-use compact solutions will enable residents to get around more easily on foot, bike, and Segway—low-cost alternatives that encourage household spending on high-quality housing.

1 Personal Rapid Transit (PRT) provides on-demand driverless travel via a dedicated guideway.

2 The United States has one-third of the world's cars. The City Car is envisioned as a space-saving personal vehicle that could reduce the impact of driving while seamlessly integrating with other modes of transit.

3 Leveraged by a public/private partnership, California's high-speed rail system will connect major cities at up to 220 miles (354 km) per hour.

4 Tysons Corner, Virginia, robust today, will be dramatically enhanced by an improved road network and four new Metrorail stations—opening up 1,700 acres (688 ha) for infill development and connecting the auto-dependent regional job center directly to both downtown Washington, D.C., and Dulles International Airport.

5 The rechargeable Segway Personal Transporter is powered by a pair of lithium-ion batteries and can travel 24 miles (38 km) or up to 480 city blocks on a single charge.

Global Car Ownership to Increase

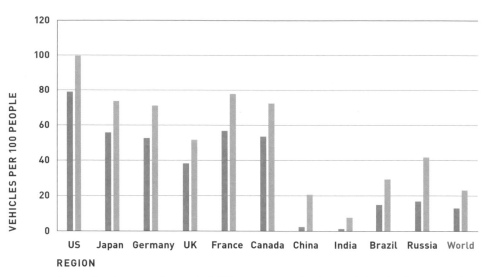

According to projections, by 2030 car ownership in most developing countries will not match that in the first world.

Source: OECD-Infrastructure 2030: Telecom, Land Transport, Water, and Electricity

Estimated Vehicle-Miles Traveled by Region in the U.S., May 2008 (in billions) and Percentage Change from 2007

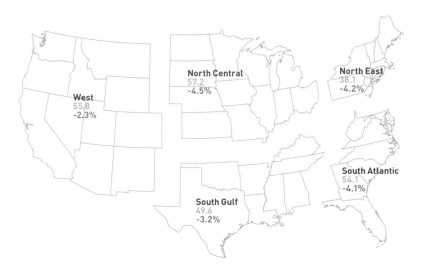

Source: U.S. Department of Transportation, 2008

Vehicle-Miles Traveled on All Roads in the U.S., 1983–2008

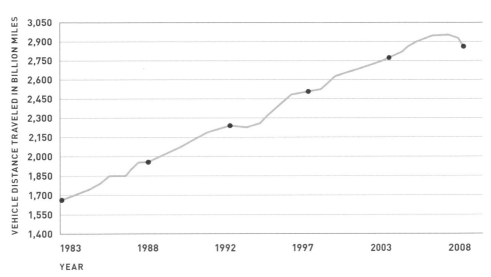

Long-term trends forecast a 48% increase in driving through 2030.
Will sustained high gas prices change this?

Source: Federal Highway Administration

Transit Ridership Surges Across the U.S.

City	% Increase	Transit Service	Date Range (approx. YTD)
Atlanta, GA	14%	MARTA Light Rail	June 2008
Charlotte, NC	34%	CATS Light Rail	January 2008
Dallas, TX	34%	DART Light Rail	Q1 2008
Denver, CO	7%	RTD Light Rail Line	Q1 2008
Miami, FL	13%	Tri-Rail Commuter Train	Q1 2008
Minneapolis, MN	16%	Hiawatha Light Rail	Q1 2008
New York City, NY	7%	New York City Subway	January 2008
San Francisco, CA	9%	Caltrain	February 2008

Sources: American Public Transportation Administration, NPR, *Dallas Morning News*

Full-Spectr

Housing

Chimney Pot Park in Salford, England, was earmarked for demolition but then adaptively transformed into high-density terraced housing.

Successful housing will mean a diversity of options. Thriving communities will provide a full spectrum of prices and types—catering to shifting demographic preferences. Buyers and renters will balance lifestyle choices with market options: retirees will downsize up the street; a family with children will move without changing schools; and employees will find homes near their jobs.

How does sea level impact property value? How do you get to work? Wh

The Perfect Fit

New definitions of "the good life" will trump floor area, lot size, and multicar garages. With average households shrinking to less than two people and elderly populations swelling, demand for smaller, more affordable homes will rise. Smaller lots and homes will mean less time lost to maintenance and money saved from rising utility payments. Parks will become backyards; restaurants and theaters will become entertainment rooms.

Fifteen Minutes to Everything

By the building or by the block, multiuse neighborhoods will provide residents with easy access to shops, recreation, places of worship, and daily services. Residents of different ages, income levels, and preferences will be supported by neighborhood retail, schools, and services—making neighborhood town centers a core building block of metropolitan growth.

Location, Location, Connection

The old adage is new again. Housing locations with easy access to destinations will drive value. Homeowners striving to control their daily schedules will put a premium on residences conveniently linked to destinations across the metropolitan region. With bus, rail, telecommuting centers, and other options, mobility-oriented communities will offer more alternatives to traffic congestion.

Design Diversity

Niche preferences will drive new forms of unit types. Small-lot townhouses, accessory rental units, starter units, generous live/work lofts, extended layouts for intergenerational living—unit variety will be the rule. And with over 20 percent of the population older than 65, there will be new markets for "assisted living" not yet invented.

Nourishing Community

Lifestyle communities will support residents with an ever-broader array of amenities and essential services. Housing will proactively integrate accessory amenities—like on-demand guest apartments, agricultural gardens, and expanded fitness centers—with redefined essential services, such as assisted living, health care, child care, and telecommute centers.

1 Harvest Lakes, a 1,000-unit community in Perth, Australia, offers well-designed smaller housing types with water-conservation and energy-efficiency features.

2 Located in Brooklyn, New York, Schaefer Landing combines 140 affordable rental units with 210 market-rate luxury condominiums.

3 On a former brownfield site in Chicago, Wentworth Commons provides 51 apartments for low-income households with easy access to transit.

4 Seattle's High Point will have 1,600 housing units for both renters and owners, creating a pedestrian-friendly neighborhood environment.

5 Urban agriculture keeps residents active and fosters community inclusion.

rms of the mortgage?   How large is the two-bedroom with in-law suite?

Housing Cost as a Percentage of Income for Renters in the U.S.

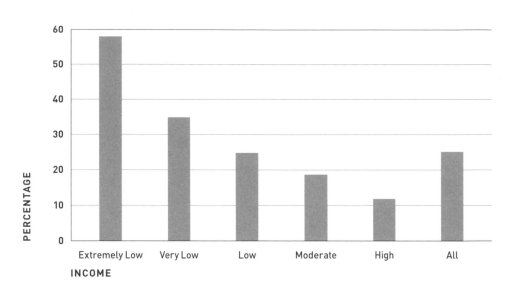

Source: Millennial Housing Commission, Meeting Our Nation's Housing Challenges, 2002

Size of Single Family Homes in the U.S.

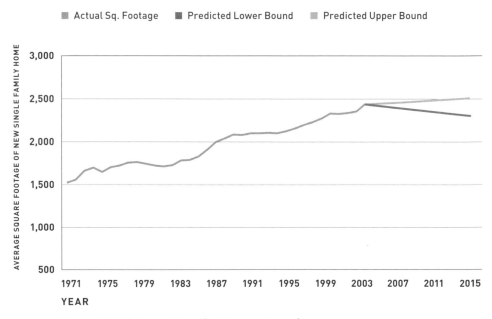

Sources: The U.S. Census Bureau (actual square footage);
National Association of Homebuilders (projected housing sizes)

Total Energy Use by Housing Type in the U.S.

■ Total Consumption (million Btu)　　■ Total U.S. Expenditures (billion dollars)　　■ Average sq/ft

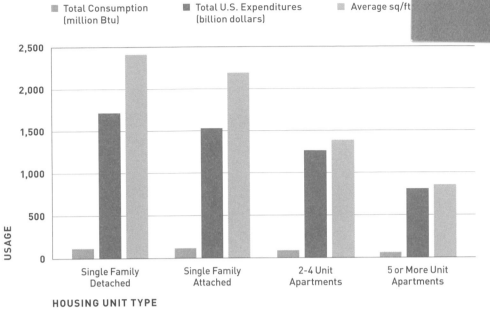

Source: Energy Information Administration, 2001

Percentage of U.S. Households by Type

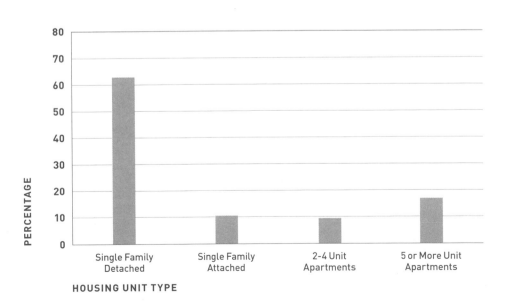

Source: Energy Information Administration, 2001

Plan It.
Build It.

Located in San Francisco Bay, the redevelopment of Treasure Island aims to remake the former Navy base as a LEED-ND certified mixed-use community. The redevelopment plan calls for nearly 60 percent of the 500-acre (81-ha) site to remain open space for recreation facilities, wildlife habitat, and local farms.

Public and private interests are aligning to develop large-scale projects. From building new cities to finding new uses for discarded sites, creative partnerships are producing lasting legacies. By sharing risks, rewards, and best practices, new large-scale developments aim at the state of the art.

How is responsible property investment measured? What is the embodied ene

Regenerate

While companies seek competitive locations, homebuyers will seek healthy lifestyles. Whole-system thinking will drive development solutions that promote sustainability and reduce costs. Wetlands will treat wastewater; runoff will recharge aquifers; methane will power buildings; and cogeneration and heat recovery will be shared between sites.

Value Sharing

When developers build with state-of-the-art technology, residents and tenants benefit. As energy, water, and waste become new profit centers, investing in innovation will require new forms of financial return. Short-term profits and long-term benefits will make ownership and value grids multidimensional.

1 Homes in Terramor, located in Orange County, California, use 20 percent less energy and water than comparable homes nearby.

2 Located on the outskirts of Shanghai, China, Dongtan will be the country's first large-scale sustainable city. By the year 2050, Dongtan will have more than 500,000 residents and will produce its own energy from a combination of renewable sources—wind, solar, and recycled municipal waste.

3 Sonoma Mountain Village, in Rohnert Park, California, will include 1,900 units, housing a total of 5,000 residents. Nearly all homes will be within a five-minute walk of the new town center.

4 Zero-carbon Masdar City outside of Abu Dhabi will provide housing for 50,000 residents, contain nearly 1,500 businesses, and create more than 70,000 jobs.

5 Located within the urban fabric of metropolitan Vienna, Flugfeld Aspern will transform a decommissioned regional airport into a 21st-century mixed-use community. At build-out, the development will contain 7,000 homes, significant office and retail space, a research campus, and a new university.

Right Sizing

Absorbing new urban dwellers demands rapid action. Whether in Asia, Europe, or the Americas, the common aim is to harness market forces to create fine-grained, livable communities. The challenge is profound, the opportunities ripe.

New Economies, New Cities

Cities are responding to economic shifts by remaking themselves. New sources of capital are coming to the table as public, private, and institutional leaders forge innovative partnerships. Johns Hopkins University remakes Baltimore with new research facilities. Wuhan becomes a new Motor City. Abu Dhabi invents a technology oasis.

Mobility Included

Sitting in traffic wastes time and fuel. Mobility will be redefined through integrated land use planning. Benefits will abound. Compact, walkable communities offering multiple transportation choices will increase access and value. High-speed rail can link cities and daily activities can be within 15-minute travel patterns.

U.S. Homeownership Rates

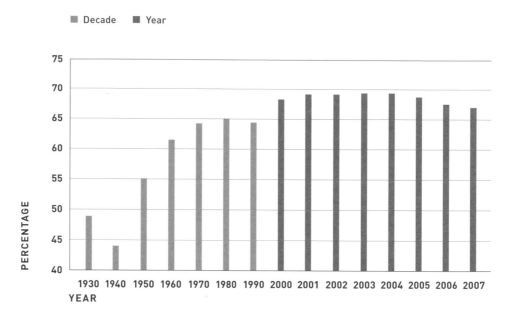

Source: The U.S. Census Bureau–Housing Vacancies and Homeownership

Sources of Newly Developed Land in the U.S.

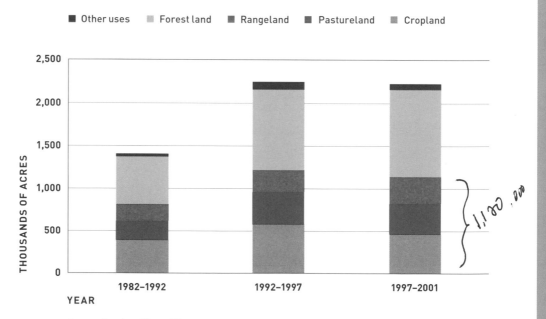

Source: Reprinted from 2001 Annual National Resources Inventory:
Urbanization and Development of Rural Land (July 2003)

Land Conservation Potential in the U.S. Under Compact Growth Scenarios, 2000–

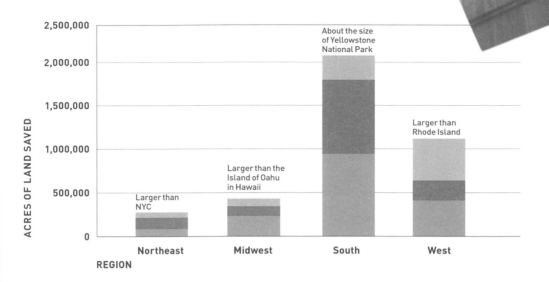

■ Agricultural Land   ■ Environmentally Fragile Lands   ■ Other

Source: Transit Cooperative Research Program, Cost of Sprawl 2000

Year Built for Existing Housing Units in the U.S.

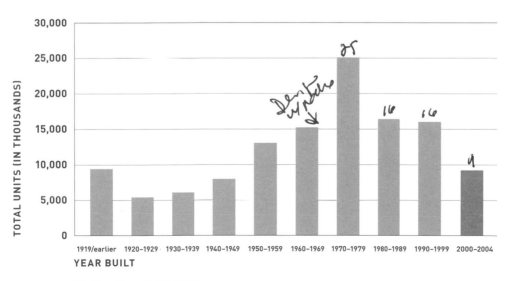

Median Year Built: 1973.

Source: The U.S. Census Bureau, 2005

Click, Learn
Go, Get.

HOUSE OF FRASER

Ireland's largest development project, Victoria Square, is located between Belfast's existing retail core and the River Lagan. Anchored by a single department store, Ireland's largest parking garage, and the largest glass dome in Europe, the project incorporated 19th-century historic buildings and civic spaces. Estimated to have 17.2 million visitors in the first year, the project boosted retail spending in the city center by 17 percent.

Evolving information technologies will create even more points of contact along the supply chain—enriching interactions between buyers and sellers. But face-to-face interaction will always be needed. Destinations for shopping, health care, culture, or education will reinvent how we shop, learn, and socialize. Accessible locations that allow buyers to "confirm" or "conclude" transactions will be robust centers of urban development.

What is the mix of retail and health care?   Where is the geopolitical risk in the s

Setting the Stage

As communities integrate a mixture of uses, a new public realm will anchor a shared urban experience. Civic spaces will rise in importance as areawide business improvement districts assume more stewardship functions to create quality destinations. Coordinated designs for both public and private spaces will transform ordinary streetscapes into uniquely branded, marketable experiences.

Knowledge Is Survival

Booming metropolitan regions will flourish with intellectual capital—with health care and education institutions at their heart. Already, these institutions drive urban development—at times employing 50 percent of a city's workforce. Professionals advancing their careers or retirees seeking lifelong learning will seek proximity to education communities. Access to world-class health care will distinguish residential markets.

Remote Access, Social Shopping

E-commerce has made its mark by moving goods from warehouses to doorsteps overnight, but the shopping trip is here to stay. Part social event, part urban experience, shopping will keep drawing people together as technology adds new twists and turns. Smart phones and navigation systems will lead eager consumers to climate-controlled gallerias, retail-retrofitted historic streets, and other "touch, try, and feel" destinations.

Pick Up or Delivery?

Origin, destination, time, and energy—the value chain of delivering products to markets will grow ever more complex. As energy and transportation costs rise, "next-day delivery" will translate to mean "from a location nearby." In central cities, large-format retail will become a mixed-use neighbor, while warehouses and "big boxes" will continue to blur at the urban edge.

Wholesale Travel

Tourism will take on a new look, as an estimated 2 billion people will enter the middle class—mostly in Asia and the Middle East. Their new disposable income and the age-old urge to explore will lead them to new destinations near and far. New cities will be built to serve this new market.

1 Aggressive marketing of urban public space extends to new programming concepts in Prague's Old Town Square.

2 The University of Maryland is driving neighborhood development around transit and retail investments, making a new town center the new center of town.

3 Search and then navigate the city to find the best in locally grown produce. Interested in fresh salmon? Try the "fresh from within 45 miles" search option on your cell phone to find vendors with local options.

4 Warehouses are as old as commerce itself, but their formats are always changing. A 1.38 million-square-foot (128,000-sq-m) warehouse in the port of Osaka, Japan, has been built up in response to the high cost of waterfront real estate.

5 How is this for cultural tourism? A Louvre museum, a Guggenheim museum, a performing arts center, a maritime museum, and a history museum built overnight. With this impressive commitment, Saadiyat Island in Abu Dhabi will make a splash in destination travel.

Should I wait and get there sooner? What are acceptable debt-to-equity ratios?

U.S. Retail Outlook: Sectors with Above Average Growth

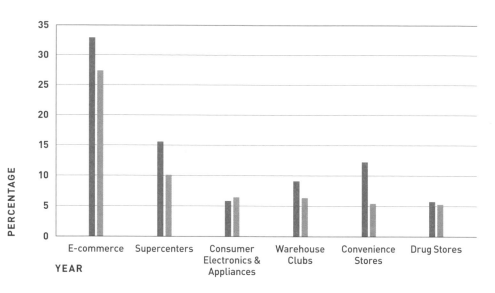

■ 2001–2006   ■ 2006–2011 (Forecast)

Source: U.S. Bureau of Economic Analysis, Retailing 2015: New Frontiers

Penetration of Devices and High-Speed Internet in U.S. Households

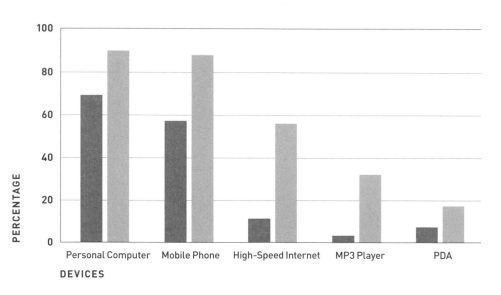

■ 2001   ■ 2006

Source: Forrester Research, Inc. and TNS Retail Forward

Personal Consumption in the U.S.: Goods vs. Services, 1980–2005

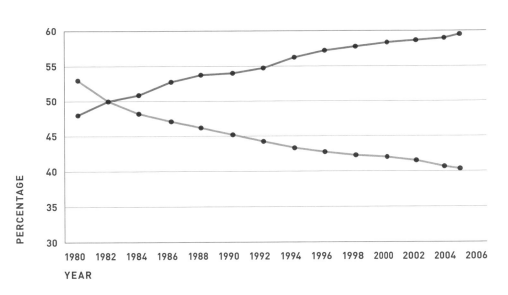

Source: U.S. Bureau of Economic Analysis, Retailing 2015: New Frontiers

Non-Auto Sales Growth Outlook, 2006–2011

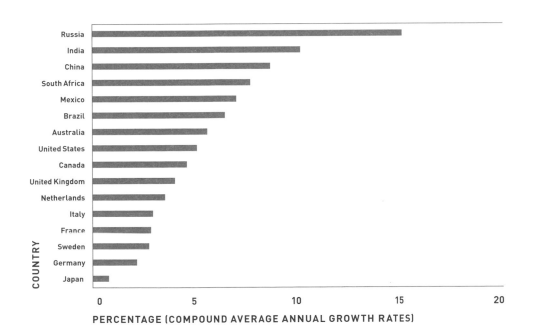

Sources: National statistics offices, OECD and TNS Retail Forward

How can to[ ]investments[ ]both attrac[ ]returns and[ ]outcomes?

ay's

achieve

ve

long-term

Housing

Reaching for 2050 will drive innovation in housing development.

What is the mix of retail and health care?

Housing

What is the embodied energy of production?

Housing

How are entitlements and permits granted?

Housing

Can kids walk to school?

Housing

Are suburbs served by light rail or rapid bus?

Infrastructure

Does it run on natural gas or hydrogen fuel cell?

Infrastructure

Infrastructure

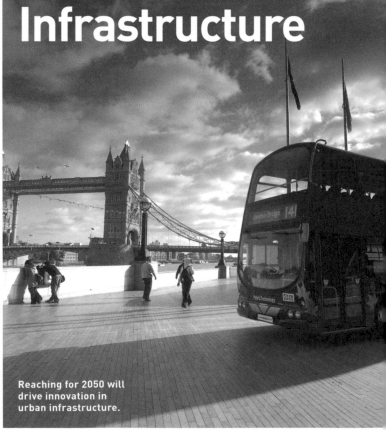

Reaching for 2050 will drive innovation in urban infrastructure.

How is the location efficiency measured?

Sustainability

Is there access to world-class health care?

Sustainability

Who is your energy conservation provider?

Sustainability

What is the indirect carbon reduction?

Sustainability

How is energy use optimized?

Infrastructure

Sustainability

Reaching for 2050 will drive innovation in developing sustainable communities.

Who owns the waste heat?

Infrastructure

What is the vehicle-to-jobs ratio?

Sustainability

How are water entitlements secured?

Sustainability

How will we
and play in 20

Age 36

**I will share
my apartment
with two college
students.**

I will pick up vegetables
from the community
garden on my way back
from the high-speed
rail station.

I will have just completed
my second PhD,
thanks to my parents'
wind energy income.

Age 45

**I will balance
my day job with
volunteer work
helping new
immigrants
living in the
neighborhood.**

I will be on the global
medical research team
for an international
university consortium
and travel to Abu Dhabi
every six months for
business strategy
meetings.

Age 14

**I will go on a
student exchange
program to
Hyderabad, India.**

I will live in the same
suburban community
my parents grew up in,
but now we have another
family living in the apartment above the garage.

I will walk to school.

ive, work,
o?

Age 30 and 4

I will drop my son off at day-care and return home to work.

I will fly on a business trip once a year to participate in the global staff retreat.

I will spend weekends walking with my son down to the town center where his 110-year-old great grandmother lives.

Age 68

I will retire and start a company that provides job re-training counseling.

I will work out of my garage, but conduct meetings at the neighborhood business center.

I will use my "wrist watch" to call the hydrogen-fueled personal mobility shuttle to get me to the golf course.

Age 91

I will finally sell that old electric-hybrid jalopy to the automobile recycling center!

I will live in a mixed-generation housing community that was developed in conjunction with the new regional clinic.

I will spend Wednesday afternoons with friends going on electric go-cart safaris in the regional park.

The Urban Land Institute convened two daylong dialogues to initiate the City in 2050 effort. These conversations revealed a remarkable diversity in the outlook for urban areas, including both optimistic views and grave concerns. This essay represents highlights from these sessions in New York City on July 22, 2008, and in San Francisco on July 29, 2008. While these initial conversations centered on the United States, other conversations will occur internationally.

**Where We've Been:
A Quick Look Back**

What can be produced in 42 years? Just look at 1966: No cell phones, BlackBerrys, or laptops; no Internet linking all corners of the Earth; far less national and international travel; homegrown businesses with a few international corporations. And in cities? People were moving to suburban communities by the hundreds of thousands, initially returning to the city for jobs and department store shopping. Suburban malls were just being built, with department stores like Montgomery Ward and Sears as primary tenants. The average American home cost approximately $25,000 (about $170,000 in 2008) and was just over 1,400 square feet (130 sq m) with one and a half bathrooms. A gallon of gas cost only 30 cents (about $2 in 2008).

In 1966, cities were sprawling outward in two general patterns: concentric circles or rings based on highway ring road construction. Think Atlanta. Or linear growth following a spine of major highways, like Highway 5 and 405 in Los Angeles. Today, most metropolitan regions are multicentered, with clear new "downtowns"—Tysons Corner in northern Virginia, Century City in Los Angeles, Buckhead in Atlanta, or the Denver Tech Center area.

The changes from 1966 to 2008 have been dramatic. In the United States alone:
□ Population has grown by over 100 million people—more than the population of New York, Chicago, Los Angeles, Denver, and Seattle combined.
□ The country has retained its title as the largest user of oil, but has moved from being the largest exporter of oil to the largest importer.
□ With a shiny new Interstate Highway System in 1966, today the United States has a $1.6 trillion infrastructure deficit, with bridges collapsing, insufficient transit, and roads full of potholes and congestion.

Rachel Carson published *Silent Spring* in 1961, giving birth to the environmental movement that is now gaining new and stronger voices worldwide. In 1963, Jane Jacobs published *The Death and Life of Great American Cities*, celebrating the diversity and grit of cities and decrying the pristine tidiness of separating land uses into separate blocks of housing, industrial, or retail. "Outdated" buildings were being demolished in the name of urban renewal, spurring the advent of the historic preservation movement.

In 2008, the suburbs have become vast cities unto themselves. Many people now live, work, and shop in the suburbs, rarely coming to the historic "downtown" or "the city." Shopping, jobs, and cultural and educational institutions followed people out to the suburbs and a new constellation was born: the metropolitan area. While the average home-to-work commute remains about 30 minutes long, it represents only about 25 percent of the trips that drivers make on American roads. All the other trips (75 percent) are the errands that come with daily life: visiting friends, shopping, picking up children, and countless other obligations that can be completed only with a car.

Metropolitan areas now span 40, 50, or more miles—in multiple directions away from the old central city. Truck traffic has increased dramatically to deliver all the goods necessary to cover such large areas. In Los Angeles, the metro area encompasses more than 600 miles; in Atlanta, over 200. Some argue that the entire Eastern Seaboard from Richmond, Virginia, to Portland, Maine, is urbanized.

From policy makers,
to young people
entering careers,
to investors choosing
portfolios, societies
will not adopt
one urban model,
but many.

Major forces will influence urban growth over the next 40 years, including population trends, energy prices, climate change, technology, and the globalization of capital.

Demographics
◻ The United States is among the fastest-growing countries in the world, with a pace of growth similar to that in China, India, and Bangladesh. In Russia and Europe, millions of people are moving to cities, but the overall populations of those areas are expected to decline.
◻ The youngest baby boomers will be 84 in another 40 years and will represent nearly 20 percent of the total population. Many will still have another 20 years of life.
◻ The percentage of people in the United States who identify as white is projected to fall from 74 to 47 percent by 2050. New definitions of how ethnicity is identified will emerge as America continues to be a melting pot and immigration keeps up.
◻ Generation Y—now in their teens and 20s—will be in their 50s and 60s and largely running the world. What will their values and goals be?
◻ Household size in the developed world is falling. In the United States, households will shrink from 2.6 persons to 2.3 by midcentury. This trend is driven by people choosing to live alone, having fewer children, and having them at older ages than previous generations.

Energy
◻ The days of cheap gas are over. Alternative fuels and more efficient cars may moderate the overall cost of driving, but the race is on to develop new vehicle technologies quickly. In the meantime, higher-priced gas is already changing people's daily driving patterns.
◻ Renewable sources of energy, nuclear, and possibly clean coal will become predominant sources of energy, gradually replacing oil and dirty coal.
◻ The overall cost of energy will rise—not just for gasoline, but for utilities as well. The amount of energy consumed by households will decline as the desire—and necessity—to buy more efficient appliances, to make older buildings more efficient, and to build new, smaller, "greener" buildings spur new innovations.

Climate Change

□ Scientists tell us that the level of greenhouse gases currently in the atmosphere will influence our lives for decades to come. Increasingly severe droughts, floods, and storms; rising sea levels; and heat islands will change how and perhaps where we live.

□ People living in coastal regions—currently half of the U.S. population—will have a decision to make: invest to protect and adapt their properties to greater climate events, or relocate.

□ The long-term migration of people in the United States from the northern to the southern and southwestern states may reverse, caused by rising temperatures and costs for air conditioning and water.

□ Legislation will increasingly constrain the use of carbon-based fuels and further raise the costs of energy and potentially limit its supply.

□ The availability of water—essential for all growth and development—may be constrained in some regions due to both increased demand and reduced availability from traditional sources.

Technology

□ The rate of change in technology, already breathtaking, will accelerate in areas such as communications, biotechnology, nanotechnology, and possibly personal transportation.

□ New technologies will not be easily predicted and the complexity of the world will make it more difficult to assess their impacts as they are delivered.

The Globalization of Capital

□ Capital will move with increasing rapidity in the global marketplace. As international funding and investing become the norm, greater volatility is expected.

□ Urban winners and losers will be chosen, both for political and economic reasons by local, regional, or national governance structures.

□ Global capital will increasingly be confounded by localized "sticky" politics as neighborhood and community organizations grow more and more sophisticated in participating in the urban development process.

Identifying Alternatives:
New Choices to Make

As the world's population grows from 6 billion to 9 billion people, more choices will face us at all levels. From policy makers, to young people entering careers, to investors choosing portfolios, societies will not adopt one urban model, but many.

Creating Civil Society

Questions persist regarding the capacity of communities to absorb changes to their core social fabric. The ability to deal with widening gaps between income groups and the challenge of absorbing large numbers of immigrants and cultures will test community resiliency. Rather than close doors, cities have always been wonderful places to share new experiences, weaving together new cultures and mixing old and new.

Creating an inclusive civil society will be different than in the past; how this process happens in a fast-paced society represents a serious challenge. We are constantly in motion; connected by

Biking, walking, and mass transit will be expanded in cities, yet the car is expected to be a permanent fixture on the road— though it is likely to look different.

dizzying communications; faced with competing stimuli from all sources; and have dramatically increased choices.

In the early 1900s, by contrast, the United States had similar growth but shared social networks provided stability. Most people went to public schools. All but the wealthiest took public transportation. People shared the same sidewalks and parks, cultural opportunities, and communications networks. Today, in an era defined by vast choice—from television stations to computer links—our cultural, educational, and recreational outlets can both relocate and then remain tied to a select community.

If the melting pot isn't the right analogy for tomorrow's metropolitan regions, then how will we foster an inclusive, productive, and resilient society? How metropolitan areas are physically built to encourage growth of civil society is a worldwide challenge today. Defining what brings people together to craft shared values and to create compatible lives in the face of great diversity is a particularly challenging problem.

Work

Where is work in the future? Historically, there was a "workplace." With greater mobility and professional specialization, some argue that "work is where you are." Communication links allow people to work from virtually anywhere. Face-to-face interaction may become more prized, and therefore, the quality—not the quantity—of meeting spaces will become more important. Will coffee shops and business centers become the new offices and conference rooms?

Which elements of the workforce need transportation? Those who commute from place to place during the workweek may change. Which service workers need to move to various locations? Will adoption of telework and shared office space mean less commuting? Education and training are already embracing remote access and redefining our campuses and universities. Scientists are collaborating across continents and time zones. To collaborate in a high-tech marketplace, labs and research facilities may require a whole new mind-set.

Retail

Who is shopping where? The Internet has opened up not only a mind-numbing amount of information, but also a world of new products. Will people do research on the Internet and then go pick up their item of choice, enabling them to see it firsthand? Or will it go the other way, where people will go try on, test out, touch, and feel items, and then go back to the Internet to shop for price?

What's the trade-off between choice and price? With an increasingly worldwide marketplace, consumers must make more conscious trade-offs between spending time shopping, browsing, researching, and exploring versus buying in a hurry.

Are stores the community gathering spots for entertainment and mixing? The role of shopping may change in society. Even more so than today, shopping may become highly segregated, where wealthy people opt for attractive stores with expensive goods and a high level of service while price-sensitive shoppers order online or in ever bigger box stores.

Transportation

Where are you going and how do you get there? Biking, walking, and mass transit will be expanded in cities, yet the car is expected to be a permanent fixture on the road—though it is likely to look different. Perhaps smaller, one-person "pod cars" will become more common, or Segways, bicycles, and scooters will have their own lane of traffic. Maybe small one- or two-person cars will become the daily driver, while larger cars are used on weekends for errands and trips out of the neighborhood. Organized car sharing may make the need to own large, infrequently used vehicles obsolete. Drivers will save money and benefit from more choice.

Movement between cities is likely to change as well. High-speed rail may make short commuter flights obsolete. Those places with great connections—at all levels, within the metropolitan region, with other nearby metro regions, and the world—will thrive, while other places with limited connections will carve out niches to compete. And perhaps a slower pace of life will be just fine for some.

By water, land, or air? By truck or train? The United States has changed from a major export nation to a major importer. Expanded seaports, inland distribution centers, and truck hubs will offer new job opportunities and present logistics planning and environmental trade-offs. The choice of transportation modes for goods also is evolving as trucks become more expensive and slower and freight trains regain competitiveness.

Housing

What do we want housing for? Of course housing provides shelter, but it has also become an entertainment center, office, and conference center. Perhaps in the future it will become a power generator or an agricultural resource. Some of these functions may move to local community centers. Growing numbers of neighborhood business centers, day-care facilities, community gardens, and education and cultural spaces may play new roles in providing that community glue to disparate groups.

Housing for all is constantly redefined with changing demographics, economic ups and downs, and new design innovations. The neighborhood is the basic community building block. How housing is stacked, shaped, interspersed with other uses, and made more efficient is a central issue for all alternative futures. The pressures of declining housing affordability and rising transportation costs will bring about a rethinking of how houses are designed and built and where they are located.

The pressures of declining housing affordability and rising transportation costs will bring about a rethinking of how houses are designed and built and where they are located.

Five Watchwords

Throughout the discussions, five words were repeated again and again: **flexibility, urgency, choice, livability, and equity.**

Flexibility is required. The pace of change is quickening. The life span of buildings and their intended use is changing. Housing often lasts over 50 years, but the number of occupants and uses change as people age, family members come and go, and different stages of life are accommodated. Commercial and retail structures may have a life span as short as five to ten years as one-story shopping gives way to larger or stacked uses. Housing over retail space is an old idea made new again today with ease of access to daily needs rising in importance. The importance of rethinking, re-creating, and reusing existing structures begs for flexible buildings, flexible use patterns, flexible citizens, and flexible cities.

Urgency is demanded to address concerns about global warming, growing populations, traffic congestion, and a restructuring of finance markets. The slowness of decision making, often cumbersome and antiquated governance structures, the inadequacy of current methods to bring together different interests to create workable compromises—all need an overhaul. Metropolitan regions can't act fast enough unless new forms of decision making are found.

Choice, a fundamental value, is both a luxury and a double-edged sword. Consumers demand choices. At all income levels and across all cultures, people seek to maximize their benefits and minimize the costs, whether measured in time, trouble, or treasure. The expansion of consumer demand for choice will require new urban laboratories that create new frameworks of "trade-offs" for personal and community decisions.

Livability is being redefined with new shapes, sizes, and patterns. Moving beyond fulfilling basic needs to achieve an enhanced quality of life is the enduring allure of urban regions, including a broad display of choices for work and a spectrum of amenities for life. But what are the thresholds of livability for ever-urbanizing populations? How do we raise the bar as millions "vote with their feet" to enhance their own livability and prosperity?

Equity raises questions of fairness in times of great change. Who gets to make decisions and what voices are heard? Many recognize that urban development can have big impacts. But will the impacts meet expectations for livability, amenities, flexibility, and individual choice? How cities and urban regions choose to share the good things in life among their many citizens will continually be played out as we move toward 2050.

The next generation of land use decisions is where all these forces come together. ULI will foster more dialogue with its members and scientists, sociologists, and others to help envision communities that are good places to live and work, competitive in a globalizing world, environmentally responsible, and welcoming to increasingly diverse populations. The City in 2050 *goes "live" in only 42 years. Please join us.*

Galbreath Family Foundation

The Galbreath Family Foundation
The City in 2050 undertaking has been made possible due to a generous donation from ULI Trustee Lizanne Galbreath on behalf of the Galbreath Family Foundation and in memory of John W. Galbreath and Daniel M. Galbreath.

Cherokee
Cherokee is a leading private equity firm investing capital and expertise in the redevelopment of urban infill sites, transit-oriented development and brownfields. For more than two decades, Cherokee's executive team has produced strong financial returns while delivering positive environmental and social results. Cherokee has invested in more than 525 properties worldwide. The firm has more than $2 billion under management and is currently investing its fourth fund. The company has evolved its leadership role in the reclamation of urban infill sites by applying expertise, creativity and resolve in sustainable redevelopment.

Akerman Senterfitt
Akerman is ranked among the top 100 law firms in the U.S. by the NLJ and is the largest firm in Florida. Comprised of more than 500 lawyers and governmental affairs professionals, our firm serves clients worldwide from 12 locations, including Miami, New York, Los Angeles, and Washington, D.C.

Bank of America
Bank of America recognizes that we have a tremendous opportunity and responsibility to address climate change through environmental initiatives that emphasize the business opportunities created by green economic growth. As a leader in community development and a champion of environmental responsibility, Bank of America has made a commitment to support the growth of environmentally sustainable business activity to address global climate change.

Cisco Systems
Cisco, (NASDAQ: CSCO), is the worldwide leader in networking that transforms how people connect, communicate and collaborate.
Information about Cisco can be found at http://www.cisco.com.
For ongoing news, please go to http://newsroom.cisco.com.

Gale International
Gale International is a premiere real estate development and investment company developing LEED-certified, master planned cities, neighborhoods and multi-use towers around the globe. Current projects in Boston include One Franklin, a $700 million, 39-story mixed use landmark tower and a $3.5 billion, 23-acre neighborhood called Seaport Square. Abroad, Gale is developing the massive 1,500 acre, $35 billion Songdo International Business District.

Miami Worldcenter
One of America's most exciting cities is giving rise to a vibrant new center. Miami Worldcenter's 12 million square feet of buildable area across 25 acres of prime real estate make it one of the largest private master-planned urban environments in the United States. With a compelling blend of mixed-use offerings in the heart of downtown, Miami Worldcenter is poised to become a magnetic, global destination.

Turnberry Group of Companies
Turnberry Associates is one of America's premier real estate development and property management companies. Founded more than 50 years ago by Donald Soffer, the company's diverse projects have revolutionized the living, working, leisure and shopping habits of millions of people across the country. The firm has to its credit the development of more than $7 billion in commercial and residential property, including approximately 20 million square feet of retail space, more than 7,000 condominium and condo-hotel residences, 1.5 million square feet of class "A" office space and in excess of 2,000 hotel and resort rooms. www.turnberry.com.

Photo Credits

The City Wild: Pages 16–21
Xochimilco Park, Mexico City, Courtesy of Grupo de Diseño Urbano
1 Courtesy of Friends of the Highline
2 Courtesy of London 2012
3 Courtesy of L.A. County Department of Public Works
4 Courtesy of Hines
5 Courtesy of Mitsui Fudosan Co, LTD

Water, Power, Light.: Pages 22–27
King Mountain Wind Ranch,
Upton County, Texas, Courtesy of Austin Energy
1 Courtesy of IDE Technologies, Ltd.
2 Courtesy of Carlos Lorenzo, Barcelona Photoblog
3 Courtesy of HTA Architects and Barratt Homes
4 Courtesy of Austin Energy
5 Courtesy of Sun Edison

Metro Metrics: Pages 28–33
Aerial Image of Vancouver, British Columbia
1 Courtesy of ULI Seattle and Mithun
2 Courtesy of Multi Corporation
3 Courtesy of San Francisco State University
4 Courtesy of Gale International
5 Courtesy of Sacramento Area Council of Governments

Whole Buildings: Pages 34–39
Bosco Verticale (Vertical Forest) in Milan, Italy, Courtesy of Studio Boeri
1 Courtesy of Adrian Smith + Gordon Gill Architecture
2 Courtesy of Harvard University Planning Office, Allston Development Group
3 Courtesy of Tise Kiester Architects, Empire Properties, and Cherokee
4 Courtesy of William McDonough and Partners
5 Courtesy of Pelli Clarke Pelli Architects, Singer Associates Inc.

Getting Around: Pages 40–45
The City Car, Courtesy of Franco Vairani/MIT Smart Cities
1 Courtesy of Advanced Transport Systems Ltd
2 Courtesy of Franco Vairani/MIT Smart Cities
3 Courtesy of California High Speed Rail Authority
4 Courtesy of Aerial Photographers, LLC
5 Courtesy of Segway

Full-Spectrum Housing: Pages 46–51
Chimney Pot Park, Courtesy of Urban Splash/Photoflex and shedkm architects
1 Courtesy of LandCorp
2 Courtesy of Kent Waterfront Associates
3 Courtesy of Enterprise Community Partners
4 Courtesy of Mithun
5 Courtesy of the Dervaes Institute

Plan It. Build It.: Pages 52–57
Treasure Island, San Francisco, CA, Courtesy of Treasure Island Community Development, LLC and SOM
1 Courtesy of Tom Lamb
2 Courtesy of Shanghai Industrial Investment Corporation and ARUP
3 Courtesy of Codding Investments
4 Courtesy of Abu Dhabi Future Energy Company and Foster + Partners
5 Courtesy of Vienna Aspern Development AG

Click, Learn, Go, Get.: Pages 58–63
Victoria Square, Belfast, Ireland, Courtesy of Building Design Partnership
1 Courtesy of Project for Public Spaces Inc.
2 Courtesy of the University of Maryland
3 Courtesy of Apple
4 Courtesy of ProLogis
5 Courtesy of Tourism Development & Investment Company

Pages 66–67
1 Multifamily housing courtyard in Malmö, Sweden, courtesy of Moore Ruble Yudell and Werner Huthmacher
2 Next-generation hybrid double-decker bus, courtesy of Transport for London
3 Tokyo Midtown, courtesy of SOM

Workshop Participants:

Michael Anikeef
Professor and Chair
Johns Hopkins University
Carey Business School
The Edward St. John
Department of Real Estate

John Alschuler
Chairman
HR&A Advisors, Inc.

Andrew Altman
Deputy Mayor for Planning and
Economic Development
City of Philadelphia

Richard Bradley
President
Downtown DC Business
Improvement District

Joe Brown
President & CEO
EDAW Inc.

Michael Buckley
Director, MSC in Real Estate and
Center for High Density Development
Columbia University

Don Carter
President
Urban Design Associates

Dan Cashdan
Co-Head Investment Banking
Holliday Fenoglio Fowler, L.P.

Stanton Eckstut
Principal
Ehrenkrantz, Eckstut &
Kuhn Architects

Barry Elbasani
President
ELS Architecture and Urban Design

Paul Freitag
Development Studio Director
Jonathan Rose Companies

Richard Gollis
Principal
The Concord Group, LLC

Bert Gregory
President & CEO
Mithun

Jim Heid
Founder
Urban Green

Rebecca Henderson
Professor
MIT Sloan School

Tara Hernandez
President
JCH Development

Mark Johnson
President
Civitas, Inc.

Chris Kurz
President & CEO
Linden Associates, Inc.

William Lashbrook
Senior Vice President
PNC Real Estate Finance

Nolan Lienhart
Associate
Zimmer Gunsul Frasca
Architects LLP

Isaac Manning
President
Trinity Works

David Mayhood
President
The Mayhood Company

James McGrath
Associate
Zimmer Gunsul Frasca
Architects LLP

Frederick Steiner
Dean, School of Architecture
UT School of Architecture

Marilyn Taylor
Partner
Skidmore, Owings & Merrill LLP

Marilee Utter
President
Citiventure Associates, LLC

Deanna Weber
Director of Sustainability
EDAW Inc.

ULI Senior Executives:

Richard M. Rosan
President, ULI Worldwide

Cheryl Cummins
President, ULI Americas

William Kistler
President, ULI Europe

David Howard
Executive Vice President,
Development & ULI Foundation

Rachelle L. Levitt
Executive Vice President,
Global Information Group

Maureen McAvey
Executive Vice President, Initiatives

Michael Terseck
Chief Financial Officer,
Chief Administrative Officer

ULI Project Staff:

Maureen McAvey
Executive Vice President, Initiatives

Uwe S. Brandes
Vice President, Initiatives

Matthew F. Johnston
Research Manager

John Miller
Scholar in Residence

ULI Senior Resident Fellows:

John K. McIlwain
Senior Resident Fellow
J. Ronald Terwilliger Chair for Housing

Michael D. Beyard
Senior Resident Fellow
ULI/Martin Bucksbaum Chair for
Retail and Entertainment

Stephen R. Blank
Senior Resident Fellow
Finance

Robert Dunphy
Senior Resident Fellow
Infrastructure and Transportation

William H. Hudnut, III
Senior Resident Fellow
ULI/Joseph C. Canizaro Chair Public Policy

Edward T. McMahon
Senior Resident Fellow
ULI/Charles Fraser Chair on
Sustainable Development

Tom Murphy
Senior Resident Fellow
ULI/Klingbeil Family Chair for
Urban Development

ULI Production Staff:

Nancy H. Stewart
Director, Book Program

David James Rose
Senior Editor

Betsy VanBuskirk
Creative Director

Craig Chapman
Director, Publishing Operations

Josh Burdick
Intern

Book and Exhibition Design:
Pentagram Design

Communications Consultant:
Garfinkel + Associates

chicago Employment growth 100% in total

Dallas 28%

Santiego 30%. [↑.61]

aug 25 mi/wk.
commuting (time) about same unece 8 a 16 mile
from home [.68]   trans't car.

Avg home 2400 SF / 2003.

Avg. US suburban density = 2,1700/ http://
www.Demographia.com /db -intlsub
html

2.59 (2010 census).

(141,235, 996 households

20%/ Ban').
10% O.P.

03

1/2 5200 × 8 = ...

a blocks

640 × 43560 = 27,878,400 SF × 0.3 = 8,363,520 SF /2,400
= 3,484.8
× 0.50 = 1,742
utilization.

2.3 DU/S / Acre
→ × 2.59 = 4,512
per SF